Let
Us
Write

365 Writing Prompts

"every beginning had to start somewhere"

An Interactive Workbook

aj houston

Not Just Alphabets Publishing

Not Just Alphabets Publishing

Fort Worth, Texas

All Not Just Alphabets Publishing titles, AJ Houston, Wordart, imprints and lines distributed are available at special quantity discounts for bulk purchases, for sales promotion, fund raising, premiums, educational, institutional and library use.

Printed in the U. S. A.

Library of Congress Catalog Card Number: 0996312927

ISBN: 978-0-9963129-2-9

Jan 28, 2023

To: Andre

Thank You for your patience. Let
me know what you think. Sorry
for the delay.

one

Dedicated:

to every one who owns a pen, pencils give you the illusion
mistakes are possible, because you can see the eraser ...

Just Write

Introduction:

In the beginning, once upon a time, remembering yester-day's, or maybe *the truth*, starting is harder than beginning. The two grouping of words used at the opening of this paragraph are the most familiar beginnings used in nearly all of the stories read to us as we were learning to read. Both of them are lead ins to let you know there is more to tell and this is just the start. Our imaginations are edgeless, there are no corners, limits or barriers to hold us back. There are miracles locked inside our heads waiting to be released. Think of it as our skin is the cage we hide the best of our thoughts under. How do you think a woman spending time alone can write the world's highest grossing novels? Or any of the male Authors, sitting in an office designing the greatest spy and sleuth novels ever written. Those are just a couple of examples of what you have inside of you.

Introductions are complicated, but let's get it over with. Hi... my name is A.J. I am a writer, well let me rephrase that; I am holder of pens learning to write. No one asked for this type of book so there is no cover story or reason it was written or thought of except for the fact it bothered me, I couldn't find one when I was looking for it. The problem with starting anything is you must have some idea of where you are planning to go. A writing prompt is simply a thought starter kit, a push uphill, downhill or whichever way you are facing to help your pen to move. There are only a few times two people has taken the same approach to any one prompt, if they had never heard someone's work utilizing it before.

I travel all over the United States working with various organizations and youth in every aspect of life, facilitating supposedly creative writing classes. I began asking myself, how creative can the writing be if I only offer my favorite genre as the exercise to learn from? Poetry... Hoping you do not look at me some type of way, I didn't answer, but I came up with the idea for this book. Every year I hear poets recycling titles from someone else's great work attempting to create great work. I have come to believe all of them found favor in the title it was created from.

A Short Story: this is also part of my introduction...

In December of 2011 I began working on a project I had doubt I would be able to finish by my targeted date. I decided to make an agreement with me, strange but true. In hopes that somewhere lying dormant in my psyche there were parts of me that would rally to my support in helping me complete it. Although I am not for sure if it happened that way but I did meet the date previously set. Then the challenge came forth... I told myself if I met the date I would write a poem for a full year, knowing at the time it took days to make words meet and agree on their placement. End of story, ever since that day I have written every day. I write something to completion, a quote, design a character for a story or a poem. We all have so many parts to us we have yet to meet, I think it is time you meet yours.

PS... not everyone likes everything of any particular artist or writer; hopefully, there are things included here you find interesting enough to follow through. Thank you for your support... *Now!* **Let Us Write.**

To start... there are things we know and many things we don't know, always believing the knowledge we have will get us through, whether learned are unlearned. Wisdom is still the application of the knowledge you possess, without the walk, the words are mere sounds, otherwise you will be considered just kind of smart or better yet school wise.

Every Beginning Had To Start Somewhere: it could be you are not a writer, but you dreamed of writing... or you are a writer, who for whatever reason, no longer possess the fire in your fingers to write... or maybe the best possible scenario: you write but not as often as you would like.

This book is for the (E) answer on every test, all of the above.

Do not let the thickness of the book challenge your psyche. You can only read one page at a time. Each prompt or exercise only requires twenty to thirty minutes of your time per day. Although, I am most positive once you discover your brain requires just as much exercise as your body, you will find delight in the releasing of your thoughts. The brain has a kind of muscle memory also, once you begin to feed it, using areas seldom used, it will automatically require more of the same for longer periods and it will take less time to accomplish what began as a chore.

No one knows for sure how much of our mind we use during any particular facet of our day, but we do know we have not used our mind to it's full potential. This is not to say these few writing exercises will do just that, truthfully; you will truly be amazed at the thoughts you are able to conjure with practice.

Thank you for accepting the challenge, not for me or from me... the challenge is yours alone. Write... write whatever you like, however you feel, whatever you think - just write... You will indeed discover you have more to say than mere words.

Come
Let Us Write

Day 1

Free write: Today write the first thing that comes to mind, when *beginning a new journey*.

_____
_____
_____
_____
_____
_____
_____
_____
_____
_____
_____
_____
_____
_____
_____
_____
_____
_____
_____
_____
_____
_____
_____
_____
_____
_____
_____
_____
_____
_____

Day 2

Write a description of you as a child, *from age 6 to age 10*, and write it in the voice of the younger you.

_____
_____
_____
_____
_____
_____
_____
_____
_____
_____
_____
_____
_____
_____
_____
_____
_____
_____
_____
_____
_____
_____
_____
_____
_____
_____
_____
_____
_____

Day 3

Write a Poem:

Describe Loving, or the act of being in love. Without Using The Word Love...

_____

_____

_____

_____

_____

_____

_____

_____

_____

_____

_____

_____

_____

_____

_____

_____

_____

_____

_____

_____

_____

_____

_____

_____

_____

_____

_____

_____

_____

_____

_____

Day 4

Write: *the Five Characteristics of Leadership*
You will have to make them up as you go.

Day 5

Write a Short Story explaining *the process of repairing a heart* you accidentally broke, include the conversation and or confrontation it will take or it took to return it to its rightful owner.

_____

_____

_____

_____

_____

_____

_____

_____

_____

_____

_____

_____

_____

_____

_____

_____

_____

_____

_____

_____

_____

_____

_____

_____

_____

_____

_____

Day 6

Look up *five new words* and write the definition from the dictionary and rewrite in your words.

_____

_____

_____

_____

_____

_____

_____

_____

_____

_____

_____

_____

_____

_____

_____

_____

_____

_____

_____

_____

_____

_____

_____

_____

_____

_____

_____

_____

_____

_____

Day 7

What is your favorite type of movie? If you were to write a movie script, what problem in the world would you want to solve or create? an action movie, sci - fi, love story, or would it be of war? or would you write of everyday life? Here's your opportunity. Today we start our treatment for a movie script. Write the concept for a movie you will eventually finish...

_____

_____

_____

_____

_____

_____

_____

_____

_____

_____

_____

_____

_____

_____

_____

_____

_____

_____

_____

_____

_____

_____

_____

_____

Day 8

Today go to a store in your area and purchase $ 10.00 - $20.00 worth of none perishables, including can goods. There are many established entities that support the surrounding community. Find the *local Food Bank* to donate the items you purchased.

_____
_____
_____
_____
_____
_____
_____
_____
_____
_____
_____
_____
_____
_____
_____
_____
_____
_____
_____
_____
_____
_____
_____
_____
_____
_____
_____
_____

Day 9

Define Quit

_____
_____
_____
_____
_____
_____
_____
_____
_____
_____
_____
_____
_____
_____
_____
_____
_____
_____
_____
_____
_____
_____
_____
_____
_____
_____
_____
_____
_____
_____

Day 10

For some projects, planning is necessary before placing pen to paper. In preparing to *Write a Play*, identify a real life situation or conversation you want to present, even if the real life didn't occur in your time line. Think of a back drop or the surrounding scenery in which this story will be transformed from thought to stage. Start your notes here:

Day 11

Write a Poem:
Once I Remember To Forget

_____

_____

_____

_____

_____

_____

_____

_____

_____

_____

_____

_____

_____

_____

_____

_____

_____

_____

_____

_____

_____

_____

_____

_____

_____

_____

_____

_____

_____

_____

Day 12

write a title for a Children's Book or Fairytale you will eventually finish. Describe the main character in detail, the objective or mission is saving a fallen dream... give the dream a name.

_____

_____

_____

_____

_____

_____

_____

_____

_____

_____

_____

_____

_____

_____

_____

_____

_____

_____

_____

_____

_____

_____

_____

_____

_____

_____

_____

_____

_____

Day 13

Write a speech of Motivation to yourself:
There Will Always Be Storms

Day 14

Today is *'Chores Day'*: perform some of the chores around the house you usually pay no attention to... wash the dishes, take out the garbage, gather the clothes to wash, cook dinner or breakfast, or visit your parents or parent house and perform the chores needed there. Happy *'Chores Day'* get to work.

Day 15

*Words **Knot Two Use** end* Place of The Write Ones:
Write at least one full paragraph using words that
sound the *same* but has a different meaning.

_____

_____

_____

_____

_____

_____

_____

_____

_____

_____

_____

_____

_____

_____

_____

_____

_____

_____

_____

_____

_____

_____

_____

_____

_____

Day 16

Today visit your local ***Children's Hospital***. There are always children who parents are working and not able to be by their side. Purchase at least three items (stuffed animals work for both sexes). Spend time with someone who welcomes the company, while there sign up and see what other things you may be able to volunteer for once a month.

_____
_____
_____
_____
_____
_____
_____
_____
_____
_____
_____
_____
_____
_____
_____
_____
_____
_____
_____
_____
_____
_____
_____
_____
_____

Day 17

Write *an original Song* to Travel by

_____

_____

_____

_____

_____

_____

_____

_____

_____

_____

_____

_____

_____

_____

_____

_____

_____

_____

_____

_____

_____

_____

_____

_____

_____

_____

_____

_____

_____

Day 18

Day 19

Explain: The Power and Problems associated with of Choice

_____

_____

_____

_____

_____

_____

_____

_____

_____

_____

_____

_____

_____

_____

_____

_____

_____

_____

_____

_____

_____

_____

_____

_____

_____

_____

_____

Day 20

Write the *Concept* to A Mystery Novel (Drama)

_____

_____

_____

_____

_____

_____

_____

_____

_____

_____

_____

_____

_____

_____

_____

_____

_____

_____

_____

_____

_____

_____

_____

_____

_____

_____

Day 21

In a Paragraph Describe Your *Favorite Bird*

_____

_____

_____

_____

_____

_____

_____

_____

_____

_____

_____

_____

_____

_____

_____

_____

_____

_____

_____

_____

_____

_____

_____

_____

_____

_____

_____

Day 22

Write a Poem:

I Am Pains Unsecret Admirer (describe not the joy of pain but the lessons you learn from going through it)

Day 23

Did You Discover Your Purpose *or when* Did Your Purpose Discover You? *Explain*

_____

_____

_____

_____

_____

_____

_____

_____

_____

_____

_____

_____

_____

_____

_____

_____

_____

_____

_____

_____

_____

_____

_____

_____

_____

Day 24

Write a *Letter to Malcom X* describing the youth of today, telling of the struggles or set backs in modern times

_____

_____

_____

_____

_____

_____

_____

_____

_____

_____

_____

_____

_____

_____

_____

_____

_____

_____

_____

_____

_____

_____

_____

_____

_____

_____

_____

_____

_____

Day 25

Write a Poem:
When Ever We...

_____

_____

_____

_____

_____

_____

_____

_____

_____

_____

_____

_____

_____

_____

_____

_____

_____

_____

_____

_____

_____

_____

_____

_____

_____

_____

_____

_____

Day 26

Write Step by Step Instructions:
How to Follow A Dream

Day 27

Write a Narrative:
A Lesson for My Children

_____

_____

_____

_____

_____

_____

_____

_____

_____

_____

_____

_____

_____

_____

_____

_____

_____

_____

_____

_____

_____

_____

_____

_____

_____

_____

_____

_____

_____

_____

_____

Day 28

Day 29

Make A List of *Things To Do Today* and Check Off
Completed Items at the End of The Day

_____

_____

_____

_____

_____

_____

_____

_____

_____

_____

_____

_____

_____

_____

_____

_____

_____

_____

_____

_____

_____

_____

_____

_____

_____

_____

_____

_____

_____

Day 30

Play Writing 101 - Challenge: Throughout your week collect one good conversation per day... repeat this exercise five times, before moving forward to the next steps for writing a Creative Stage Play. Think back to the most interesting conversation you've had in the past week. What was the main topic or *reoccurring theme* of that conversation? What was the lasting phrase or statement that stuck with you from that conversation? Chances are if it stuck with you it will stick with others. *(This is the title of your work!)*

Day 31

Look up *five new words* and write the definition from the dictionary and rewrite in your words.

_____

_____

_____

_____

_____

_____

_____

_____

_____

_____

_____

_____

_____

_____

_____

_____

_____

_____

_____

_____

_____

_____

_____

_____

_____

_____

_____

Beginning anything is hard

sticking to anything is hard

writing everything is hard

it depends on

how much you want to remember

and how much you are willing

to sacrifice

in remembrance...

Day 32

For the opening scene of your movie… where will it take place? What time of day? What's the weather like? What is the background or back drop? What will the opening dialog be? Will it be a voice over, or a conversation of one or more of the characters?

Day 33

Write a Poem or Story: telling the next person you
meet of your intentions…

_____
_____
_____
_____
_____
_____
_____
_____
_____
_____
_____
_____
_____
_____
_____
_____
_____
_____
_____
_____
_____
_____
_____
_____
_____
_____
_____
_____
_____
_____
_____
_____

Day 34

Write a Short Story: depicting the child in you instructing the now you, being and doing what you have always dreamed of...

_____

_____

_____

_____

_____

_____

_____

_____

_____

_____

_____

_____

_____

_____

_____

_____

_____

_____

_____

_____

_____

_____

_____

_____

_____

_____

_____

Day 35

Make plans to visit the *National Museum of History*, take your time while there to view and learn something you only before thought you knew.

_____

_____

_____

_____

_____

_____

_____

_____

_____

_____

_____

_____

_____

_____

_____

_____

_____

_____

_____

_____

_____

_____

_____

_____

_____

_____

_____

_____

_____

_____

_____

Day 36

Men Are Made Of...

_____

_____
_____

_____
_____

_____
_____

_____
_____

_____
_____

_____
_____

_____
_____

_____
_____

_____
_____

_____
_____

_____
_____

_____
_____

_____
_____

_____

Day 37

Describe in detail your process from conception to fruition of *whatever you create*... a poem, short story, play, movie script, painting... make it clear, use a chart or diagram if needed...

Day 38

Using your favorite Animal of The Jungle, Write a *Poem or Short Story* From it's Point of View

Day 39

Some Days I Run Away *from / to* Myself. Choose one...
Explain why

_____

_____

_____

_____

_____

_____

_____

_____

_____

_____

_____

_____

_____

_____

_____

_____

_____

_____

_____

_____

_____

_____

_____

_____

Day 40   Write a *Rap Song* about Your Favorite Item of Clothing

_____

_____

_____

_____

_____

_____

_____

_____

_____

_____

_____

_____

_____

_____

_____

_____

_____

_____

_____

_____

_____

_____

_____

_____

_____

_____

_____

_____

Day 41

What is it made of or Define: *Success?*

Day 42

every main character has a sidekick or best friend: describe in detail the sidekick for your character you created for your children's book or fairytale. How it looks, speak and the quirky characteristics it brings to the story.

_____

_____

_____

_____

_____

_____

_____

_____

_____

_____

_____

_____

_____

_____

_____

_____

_____

_____

_____

_____

_____

_____

_____

_____

_____

Day 43

Write a Song *dedicated to* The Rain

Day 44

Find an organization in your area that has a *year round toy drive,* follow the process listed to donate. Not everyone waits until the holidays to show love and support. It doesn't take a lot of money to do so. If you can't find one set up one with your friends and family, it is ok to start small. All help is welcomed and needed.

Day 45

Look up *five new words* and write the definition from the dictionary and rewrite in your words.

Day 46

Write A Recipe For Love... Include at least Eight Ingredients and Detail the cooking Instructions and use for each...

_____

_____

_____

_____

_____

_____

_____

_____

_____

_____

_____

_____

_____

_____

_____

_____

_____

_____

_____

_____

_____

_____

_____

_____

_____

_____

_____

Day 47

Day 48

In Your Garden You Are **Growing Purpose:** Describe the Process For Planting, Nurturing and How Deep You Must Dig For Purpose To Grow...

Day 49

Write A Letter To The Little Boy or Girl In You

Day 50

Teachings From My Father

_____

_____

_____

_____

_____

_____

_____

_____

_____

_____

_____

_____

_____

_____

_____

_____

_____

_____

_____

_____

_____

_____

_____

_____

_____

_____

_____

_____

Day 51

_____
_____
_____
_____
_____
_____
_____
_____
_____
_____
_____
_____
_____
_____
_____
_____
_____
_____
_____
_____
_____
_____
_____
_____
_____
_____
_____
_____

Day 52

Write a ***Thank You letter*** to the Parents or Parent Who Raised You

_____

_____

_____

_____

_____

_____

_____

_____

_____

_____

_____

_____

_____

_____

_____

_____

_____

_____

_____

_____

_____

_____

_____

_____

_____

_____

_____

_____

_____

_____

Day 53

_____
_____
_____
_____
_____
_____
_____
_____
_____
_____
_____
_____
_____
_____
_____
_____
_____
_____
_____
_____
_____
_____
_____
_____
_____
_____
_____

Day 54

Write a Poem:
And We Still Cry For Justice

_____

_____

_____

_____

_____

_____

_____

_____

_____

_____

_____

_____

_____

_____

_____

_____

_____

_____

_____

_____

_____

_____

_____

_____

_____

_____

Day 55

There are thousands of **Boys and Girls Clubs,** locate the one nearest you and see what opportunities they have available. Sign up to donate a couple of hours once a month. There are youth around you in need of moral support and guidance.

_____

_____

_____

_____

_____

_____

_____

_____

_____

_____

_____

_____

_____

_____

_____

_____

_____

_____

_____

_____

_____

_____

_____

_____

_____

_____

_____

Day 56

I Would Follow You To...
(Nowhere if it was a place, *Everywhere*, *Forever* or make up your own destination)

_____

_____

_____

_____

_____

_____

_____

_____

_____

_____

_____

_____

_____

_____

_____

_____

_____

_____

_____

_____

_____

_____

_____

_____

_____

_____

_____

_____

Day 57

What Are *The Benefits* of Friendship?

Day 58

For your Stage play: Write down the names and a brief description of all the characters that were involved in that conversation. *(This is your cast of characters!)* Write a brief description of the place in which this conversation took place. Were you at a local coffee shop on a lazy Sunday afternoon, speaking with another customer amidst the sound of espresso machines, with smooth jazz playing in the background? or was it a crowded nightclub? *(This is your setting and set description!)*

when dreamers marry pens

secretly

you don't have to tell...

others will notice

how pen stays close

witness the indentations

on your fingers

they will grasp it in the way

your words feel

when they read them

it is always easier to see

how love looks

in the books you write

no need to tell

your words

will speak

for themselves

Day 59

I Learned *Everything I Know* From…

_____

_____

_____

_____

_____

_____

_____

_____

_____

_____

_____

_____

_____

_____

_____

_____

_____

_____

_____

_____

_____

_____

_____

_____

_____

_____

_____

_____

_____

_____

_____

_____

_____

Day 60

Write a Short Story detailing the adventure of walking to the store or market, *list the trials* of getting there, arriving back home to prepare a meal. Write how each dish being served was prepared. Use your imagination.

_____

_____

_____

_____

_____

_____

_____

_____

_____

_____

_____

_____

_____

_____

_____

_____

_____

_____

_____

_____

_____

_____

_____

_____

_____

_____

_____

Day 61

For your movie… what is the name of the main character? Is it male or female? Create the background history, how are they dressed? are they wealthy, working class or poor? Detail the opening scene or situation, include the number of extras needed, are they in motion? Plane, train, car, boat, bicycle, running? *Describe every element.*

Day 62

Somewhere In The Dark of Night

Day 63

Write An Argument Proving Love Is Blind...

Day 64

What Is The *Hardest Temptation* for You To Resist?

_____

_____

_____

_____

_____

_____

_____

_____

_____

_____

_____

_____

_____

_____

_____

_____

_____

_____

_____

_____

_____

_____

_____

_____

_____

Day 65

Write a clear *Definition of Hope...*

Day 66

Check online or the local event page of the newspaper to ***find a local artist*** having a show of his / her paintings. Go to the art show and enjoy. ***Culture time...*** there are great unknown painters living amongst us.

Day 67

Write the names of the people and a list of the things *In Order,* as they occurred at Your Favorite Birthday Celebration...

_____

_____

_____

_____

_____

_____

_____

_____

_____

_____

_____

_____

_____

_____

_____

_____

_____

_____

_____

_____

_____

_____

_____

_____

_____

_____

Day 68

Look up *five new words* and write the definition from the dictionary and rewrite in your words.

_____

_____

_____

_____

_____

_____

_____

_____

_____

_____

_____

_____

_____

_____

_____

_____

_____

_____

_____

_____

_____

_____

_____

_____

_____

_____

_____

_____

_____

Day 69

Write a *Poem or Short Story* about A Law You Would Like to see Changed

_____

_____

_____

_____

_____

_____

_____

_____

_____

_____

_____

_____

_____

_____

_____

_____

_____

_____

_____

_____

_____

_____

_____

_____

_____

_____

_____

_____

Day 70

Day 71

If Life was a *Snooze Button:* How many times do you *push / pause* it? and How do you Wake Up!

_____

_____

_____

_____

_____

_____

_____

_____

_____

_____

_____

_____

_____

_____

_____

_____

_____

_____

_____

_____

_____

_____

_____

_____

_____

_____

_____

Day 72

Write Your *Theory of Love*

_____

_____

_____

_____

_____

_____

_____

_____

_____

_____

_____

_____

_____

_____

_____

_____

_____

_____

_____

_____

_____

_____

_____

_____

_____

_____

Day 73

When *All Else* Fails…

_____
_____
_____
_____
_____
_____
_____
_____
_____
_____
_____
_____
_____
_____
_____
_____
_____
_____
_____
_____
_____
_____
_____
_____
_____
_____
_____
_____
_____
_____

Day 74

give your villain or problem a name and description: one it will maintain throughout the children's book or fairytale, even if it is to play more than one role in the story.

_____

_____
_____
_____
_____
_____
_____
_____
_____
_____
_____
_____
_____
_____
_____
_____
_____
_____
_____
_____
_____
_____
_____
_____
_____
_____

Day 75

Describe a *Far Away Place* either Imagined or Real

_____

_____

_____

_____

_____

_____

_____

_____

_____

_____

_____

_____

_____

_____

_____

_____

_____

_____

_____

_____

_____

_____

_____

_____

_____

_____

_____

_____

_____

_____

_____

_____

_____

Day 76

Write *Both Sides of The Debate* To Be or Not To Be...
To Give Up or Stay In The Fight...

_____

_____

_____

_____

_____

_____

_____

_____

_____

_____

_____

_____

_____

_____

_____

_____

_____

_____

_____

_____

_____

_____

_____

_____

_____

_____

_____

Day 77

Describe the emotion Anger...

_____

_____

_____

_____

_____

_____

_____

_____

_____

_____

_____

_____

_____

_____

_____

_____

_____

_____

_____

_____

_____

_____

_____

_____

_____

_____

_____

_____

_____

_____

Day 78

15 Things I Need To Say Before I Lose My Nerves...

_____
_____
_____
_____
_____
_____
_____
_____
_____
_____
_____
_____
_____
_____
_____
_____
_____
_____
_____
_____
_____
_____
_____
_____
_____
_____
_____
_____

Day 79

Write an *action Poem or Short Story* where each line or verse is filled with motion… ie.. Jumping rope, cliff diving, parachuting, running, falling, etc...

_____

_____

_____

_____

_____

_____

_____

_____

_____

_____

_____

_____

_____

_____

_____

_____

_____

_____

_____

_____

_____

_____

_____

_____

_____

_____

_____

_____

Day 80

Make A List of The *Top Twenty Excuses* You Have
Ever Used To Get Out of Doing Something...

Day 81

I Am Most *Creative and Alive* When I Am…

_____
_____
_____
_____
_____
_____
_____
_____
_____
_____
_____
_____
_____
_____
_____
_____
_____
_____
_____
_____
_____
_____
_____
_____
_____
_____
_____
_____
_____
_____
_____
_____

Day 82

Write one paragraph *of motivational thoughts* to get you through the challenges of your day...

Day 83

Write a Poem: *Pieces Of Never*

Day 84

For your movie... describe the friends, family and adversaries of the main character, define the roles they will play as the story moves forward.

Day 85

Locate your local ***Community Outreach Program***, inquire what services they provide, sign up to participate, it will only require a couple of hours per month. Or maybe you can purchase and supply some of the items they pass out.

I am honored you made it this far

I applaud you for your follow through

If you have ever watched any sports

Cheerleaders are a big part

for audience participation

I am your cheering section

Keep up the great work

Write

Day 86

Trapped Inside *My Yesterdays*

_____
_____
_____
_____
_____
_____
_____
_____
_____
_____
_____
_____
_____
_____
_____
_____
_____
_____
_____
_____
_____
_____
_____
_____
_____
_____
_____
_____
_____

Day 87

For your Stage play: think back to all the strange objects that were used by the participants in this conversation. Did the person who approached you in the nightclub already have a glass in his / her hand? Was the customers in the coffee shop reading the newspaper when you approached to ask the time? (*The items you add will be your Props List!)*

Day 88 Describe The *Dividing Line* Between Pain and Purpose…

Day 89

Write a Short Story of children *playing a card game*, you can make up your own game with whatever rules you would like, but they are gambling, instead of money they offer their parents and other members of their family *as revenue.*

Day 90

Scavenger Hunt:
Hide Something You Treasure: draw a detailed **Map** with highlighted areas, attach written instructions, include a diagram, and Give It to the Person You Love

Day 91

Look up *five new words* and write the definition from the dictionary and rewrite in your words.

Day 92

Poetry has been around for centuries, find a *local open mic or slam* to visit and listen to life spoken.

_____

_____

_____

_____

_____

_____

_____

_____

_____

_____

_____

_____

_____

_____

_____

_____

_____

_____

_____

_____

_____

_____

_____

_____

_____

_____

_____

Day 93

Write: The *Story of* My Life

Day 94

Describe the *most beautiful scenery* or the most serene place you have ever been or thought of going...

_____

_____

_____

_____

_____

_____

_____

_____

_____

_____

_____

_____

_____

_____

_____

_____

_____

_____

_____

_____

_____

_____

_____

_____

_____

_____

Day 95 Look up and write the *actual functions* of the heart muscle

_____

_____

_____

_____

_____

_____

_____

_____

_____

_____

_____

_____

_____

_____

_____

_____

_____

_____

_____

_____

_____

_____

_____

_____

_____

_____

_____

Day 96

Lessons from My mother

Day 97

Read a poem or story *you wrote earlier* in life, rewrite it to see how or if you have grown in your process of combing ideas…

Day 98

What Makes *A Family?*

_____

_____

_____

_____

_____

_____

_____

_____

_____

_____

_____

_____

_____

_____

_____

_____

_____

_____

_____

_____

_____

_____

_____

_____

_____

_____

_____

_____

_____

_____

_____

_____

Day 99

Write a Poem: You Are My Outside In

Day 100

the local ***Battered Women's Shelter*** in your area could always use daily necessities, either for the shelters use or the families visiting. Check to see what items they are in need of, purchase the items you can afford and drop them off. There may be others services you could perform, try and donate an hour or two a month to help out.

Day 101

Day 102

Write a paragraph detailing the order *from start to finish* of something exploding... attitude, dynamite, nitroglycerin, relationship...

_____

_____

_____

_____

_____

_____

_____

_____

_____

_____

_____

_____

_____

_____

_____

_____

_____

_____

_____

_____

_____

_____

_____

_____

_____

_____

_____

_____

_____

Day 103

The Things *I Still Struggle* with…

Day 104

In the House Where I *Grew Up*

_____
_____
_____
_____
_____
_____
_____
_____
_____
_____
_____
_____
_____
_____
_____
_____
_____
_____
_____
_____
_____
_____
_____
_____
_____
_____
_____
_____

Day 105

Build the character of the **adversary or villain in Your Movie**... the character must be loved first, in order to be hated, start with all of the good traits, show the adversary having great adoration for the human condition is what drove him / her to **such desperate measures** of destruction, and complete the description with a list of fatal flaws.

Day 106

The *Melody* in *Your Eyes*

Day 107

If You Wrote A *How To Book*... What Would You Teach?

_____
_____
_____
_____
_____
_____
_____
_____
_____
_____
_____
_____
_____
_____
_____
_____
_____
_____
_____
_____
_____
_____
_____
_____
_____

Day 108

for the children's book or fairytale: describe at least three additional sub characters and the specific places they will appear in the telling of the story or the roles they will play. This is needed to add color and or flavor to create a well-rounded story.

_____
_____
_____
_____
_____
_____
_____
_____
_____
_____
_____
_____
_____
_____
_____
_____
_____
_____
_____
_____
_____
_____
_____
_____
_____

Day 109

Write a Poem:
and there was **Blues** playing in the **Background**

Day 110

_____
_____
_____
_____
_____
_____
_____
_____
_____
_____
_____
_____
_____
_____
_____
_____
_____
_____
_____
_____
_____
_____
_____
_____
_____
_____
_____
_____

Day 111

Write A Short Story About Your *Favorite Things…*
(include at least five things)

Day 112

Everything You Need to *Know* about *Me*...

there is always

an answer

even if the question

never existed

or has yet

to gather

enough motion

or volume

to become

audible

Day 113

When You *Make It Through* The Storm

Day 114

Plan A Day With In The Coming Week to *Visit A Place* In Your City you have wanted to go, but have *Never Been...* go and Write About It...

_____

_____

_____

_____

_____

_____

_____

_____

_____

_____

_____

_____

_____

_____

_____

_____

_____

_____

_____

_____

_____

_____

_____

_____

_____

_____

_____

_____

Day 115

For you Stage play: write down the conversation as you remember it word for word. Remember what made this conversation interesting to you, be sure to add the significance needed to highlight those moments. The only tool you have to do this is PUNCTUATION. Use exclamations point to create excitement, commas to add necessary pauses, ellipses to provide spaces for your characters to sit in silence and think. *(This is your Character Dialogue!)*

Day 116

Write a Poem:
The ***First Time I Listened*** To Your Heart Beat

_____
_____
_____
_____
_____
_____
_____
_____
_____
_____
_____
_____
_____
_____
_____
_____
_____
_____
_____
_____
_____
_____
_____
_____
_____
_____
_____
_____
_____

Day 117

Somewhere away from here, *nowhere* but here, *anywhere* will still be here... make the point of why *Here* matters... letting *Here* be your *Now*.

Day 118

Refrigerate After Opening... Write a Description of a Long Term *Goal or Endeavor* You Want to Keep Fresh as You Move it Toward Fruition

Day 119

If You Were A Doctor, You Would *Find A Cure For*
_____... Explain what it is and
why this is your choice.

_____

_____

_____

_____

_____

_____

_____

_____

_____

_____

_____

_____

_____

_____

_____

_____

_____

_____

_____

_____

_____

_____

_____

_____

_____

Day 120

Look up *five new words* and write the definition from the dictionary and rewrite in your words.

Day 121

Locate; if you are not familiar with where it is, The *Main Library* in your city. Sign up for a library card and check out a book. There has to be something there you find interesting.

Day 122

Write A Short Story or Poem about *A Family Heirloom* that has been Passed Down for Generations

Day 123

Write the Instructions *In Order*, How To *Build a Wall*... List The Parts Of You To Keep Behind It...

Day 124

List All the Items You Would Keep In *A Box of Promise*

_____
_____
_____
_____
_____
_____
_____
_____
_____
_____
_____
_____
_____
_____
_____
_____
_____
_____
_____
_____
_____
_____
_____
_____

Day 125

The *Day* We *Met*

_____

_____

_____

_____

_____

_____

_____

_____

_____

_____

_____

_____

_____

_____

_____

_____

_____

_____

_____

_____

_____

_____

_____

_____

_____

_____

_____

_____

_____

_____

_____

Day 126

Write or Create *Six Steps* for Building *Confidence* and or *Self Esteem*

_____

_____

_____

_____

_____

_____

_____

_____

_____

_____

_____

_____

_____

_____

_____

_____

_____

_____

_____

_____

_____

_____

_____

Day 127

There Is A War Raging, on *The Same Street* I Used Live…

Day 128

Write a Poem describing the music of an orchestra, listing *the Instruments* of the *Orchestra* you used To Create It

_____

_____

_____

_____

_____

_____

_____

_____

_____

_____

_____

_____

_____

_____

_____

_____

_____

_____

_____

_____

_____

_____

_____

_____

_____

_____

_____

_____

Day 129

What and When Was Your Last Act of Persistence?
Why Did it or Didn't it Work? *(explain)*

Day 130

There are church affiliated organization and non-religious entities performing acts of kindness, *feeding the homeless,* setting up in parks to give families a safe outing. Find those in your area and donate, food, toys, or help in the areas they need support with specifically.

Day 131

After The Kiss

Day 132

Peace isn't always *discovered in quiet*, sometimes it is located in the midst of chaos... where do you go to find Peace?

_____

_____

_____

_____

_____

_____

_____

_____

_____

_____

_____

_____

_____

_____

_____

_____

_____

_____

_____

_____

_____

_____

_____

_____

_____

Day 133

For Those Who *Have Gone* Before...

_____

_____

_____

_____

_____

_____

_____

_____

_____

_____

_____

_____

_____

_____

_____

_____

_____

_____

_____

_____

_____

_____

_____

_____

_____

_____

_____

_____

Day 134

If Feelings are the Union of Thoughts and Emotions.
Define Emotions...

Day 135

for your movie... write a series of possible conversations between the main character and the adversary, showing there is a mutual understanding of their roles, and build a type of respect between the two characters... the best conflict comes through understanding what you are up against.

Day 136

Write Your Actual *Job Description* include *All The Responsibilities* You Have on Your Job... even those that were not included when you were hired.

Day 137

For Your Stage play: think back to all the facial/vocal expressions and physical movements your characters did in an effort to convey their points or as a part of their habitual human interacting. Re-read your dialogue and insert these actions in parentheses (*using italics*). *(These are your Stage Directions/Physical Dialogue!)*

Day 138

Day 139

If You Had *A Magic Key.* What Door Would It Open? and *why* was it locked?

_____

_____

_____

_____

_____

_____

_____

_____

_____

_____

_____

_____

_____

_____

_____

_____

_____

_____

_____

_____

_____

_____

_____

_____

_____

Day 140

Create a list of obstacles, or problems (at least two) for the main character and sidekick of your Children's Book or Fairytale will eventually solve:

Day 141

The Gift of You...

_____

_____

_____

_____

_____

_____

_____

_____

_____

_____

_____

_____

_____

_____

_____

_____

_____

_____

_____

_____

_____

_____

_____

_____

_____

_____

_____

_____

_____

_____

_____

Day 142

There is Glow or a Light *At The End* of The
Tunnel... Describe it and its origin

Day 143

I've Found *Hidden Treasure* In Your Smile…

_____

_____

_____

_____

_____

_____

_____

_____

_____

_____

_____

_____

_____

_____

_____

_____

_____

_____

_____

_____

_____

_____

_____

_____

_____

_____

_____

_____

Today expand your mind beyond the borders and perimeters you believed were set... in other words, destroy the proverbial box / system / traditional processes you have become used to. Use your imagination to imagine, there was never a box - and your new Truth is: everything has always been limitless.

Day 144

In Your Most *Imaginative Tirade,* Explain What Kisses *Are Made Of*

Day 145

Search online for the *Meals on Wheels* location supporting your community, go through the process to sign up to drive once a month. There are *lessons in helping* you can't receive from looking from a distance. Fill out the form, *and follow through.*

_____

_____

_____

_____

_____

_____

_____

_____

_____

_____

_____

_____

_____

_____

_____

_____

_____

_____

_____

_____

_____

_____

_____

_____

Day 146

Look up *five new words* and write the definition from the dictionary and rewrite in your words.

_____

_____

_____

_____

_____

_____

_____

_____

_____

_____

_____

_____

_____

_____

_____

_____

_____

_____

_____

_____

_____

_____

_____

_____

_____

_____

_____

Day 147

Write The Instructions on How To: ***Build A Bridge*** From ***Disappointment*** To ***Satisfaction***...

Day 148

Imagine the type of boat you would set sail on, describe it, *create an island or choose one* of the many already in existence to sail away to... *write of the journey* using navigational terms, include how long it will take to arrive at your destination, add at least *one storm* encountered during the journey.

Day 149

Describe A *Day* Without Your *Cell Phone* or *Tablet.*

Day 150

Write a Poem:
I'll Be Here Waiting

Day 151

Viewing the downtown area during your drive to and from work makes it look interesting from the distance. *Spend an evening downtown*, walk around to find what's new or rediscover something old. Have dinner in a restaurant you have never visited, eat something new. *Enjoy your Downtown Excursion.*

Day 152

We celebrate our accomplishments, in games of chance, in sports, receiving accolades of all types... ***Discuss*** where you find your inner Victories to help you keep moving, motivated or even to keep standing...*"I Found Victory When"*

_____

_____

_____

_____

_____

_____

_____

_____

_____

_____

_____

_____

_____

_____

_____

_____

_____

_____

_____

_____

_____

_____

_____

_____

_____

_____

_____

Day 153 *Define:* The *Unbreakable Bond* of *Brothers / Sisters*

Day 154

If You Were A Cloud, *What Shape* Would You Form and What could You See from up high?

_____
_____
_____
_____
_____
_____
_____
_____
_____
_____
_____
_____
_____
_____
_____
_____
_____
_____
_____
_____
_____
_____
_____

Day 155

Write *a Detailed Description* of Your Favorite Picture of Someone Other Than Yourself, include the particulars... background, hair color, eye color, shapes and contours of face and nose, etc...

Day 156

Define Light without using the word light

_____

_____

_____

_____

_____

_____

_____

_____

_____

_____

_____

_____

_____

_____

_____

_____

_____

_____

_____

_____

_____

_____

_____

_____

_____

_____

_____

_____

_____

_____

Day 157

Write a *Pitch* To Yourself, *for the Business* you will soon run or the one you Plan to Start…

_____

_____
_____
_____
_____
_____
_____
_____
_____
_____
_____
_____
_____
_____
_____
_____
_____
_____
_____
_____
_____
_____
_____
_____
_____
_____
_____
_____

Day 158

Spelunkers Explore Deep Caverns in The Earth…
if **Love Was A Cave**, What Would You Find and
How Would You Excavate It?

_____

_____

_____

_____

_____

_____

_____

_____

_____

_____

_____

_____

_____

_____

_____

_____

_____

_____

_____

_____

_____

_____

_____

_____

_____

_____

_____

Day 159

Define Promise...

_____

_____
_____
_____
_____
_____
_____
_____
_____
_____
_____
_____
_____
_____
_____
_____
_____
_____
_____
_____
_____
_____
_____
_____
_____
_____
_____

Day 160

Write the History of your family or what you know of Your *Genealogy and Family Tree.*

_____

_____

_____

_____

_____

_____

_____

_____

_____

_____

_____

_____

_____

_____

_____

_____

_____

_____

_____

_____

_____

_____

_____

_____

_____

_____

_____

_____

_____

Day 161

Dear Veteran: Write a Letter Thanking Them for Their Service

Day 162

Write a Short Story detailing *the process* and *origin of rain*, where it comes from, *why it falls*, where it goes after it lands, make it up if you have to.

Day 163

Write Down or (Chart) The Amount of Time *(minutes or hours)* You Spend on Your *Phone, Tablet, Computer* Not Being Productive... *(List One Day and Multiply it Times 365)*

Day 164

Describe an Imaginary Rendezvous You Would Like To Have… (with a person, you don't have to name, use your imagination)

Day 165

For your Stage play: review the dialog of your characters… make sure *each character* plays a focused role in the story, no reason for a long build up, *get to the point.* Write the c*onflict,* let each character show what is at stake… present a clear point or objective for each interaction. The *conflict* has to have *a beginning, middle and an end…* work your way there.

Day 166

Write a note describing to the Present You what to expect before the Arrival of Tomorrow, include a warning of what must be done to make it through the coming day.

Day 167

I Discovered *Lost Pieces* of Me In...

_____
_____
_____
_____
_____
_____
_____
_____
_____
_____
_____
_____
_____
_____
_____
_____
_____
_____
_____
_____
_____
_____
_____
_____
_____
_____
_____
_____
_____
_____

Day 168

Women Are Made Of...

_____

_____

_____

_____

_____

_____

_____

_____

_____

_____

_____

_____

_____

_____

_____

_____

_____

_____

_____

_____

_____

_____

_____

_____

_____

_____

_____

_____

_____

_____

Day 169

for your movie... write the scene in which the adversary first appears on screen. Is the adversary wealthy, working class or poor? Give the *back story* of how he / she came to be in the present state. Where are they, office, board room, factory floor, club / bar, walking alone or with someone? Will the dialog presented be a *voice over*, a historical review of past occurrences? Write in *all the details*.

Day 170

Define *Darkness*

_____

_____

_____

_____

_____

_____

_____

_____

_____

_____

_____

_____

_____

_____

_____

_____

_____

_____

_____

_____

_____

_____

_____

_____

_____

_____

_____

_____

_____

_____

_____

Day 171

Write a Poem:
Something *I Need to Say* before I Forget

Day 172

Research: Find the ***Origin*** of Your Favorite Story or Parable in the Bible, find if there are other paralleling ***stories similar*** and which one came first...

_____

_____

_____

_____

_____

_____

_____

_____

_____

_____

_____

_____

_____

_____

_____

_____

_____

_____

_____

_____

_____

_____

_____

_____

_____

_____

_____

Day 173

Obstacle or Problem 1 for your children's book or fairytale: identify the item or items and write how it / they occur, or under what circumstances it comes about, detail the *exact solution* the main character and sidekick will use in *accomplishing* the mission.

Day 174

What would be *the easiest to fulfill*, a Bundle of *Dreams*, a Bouquet of *Wishes* or a Pocket Full of *Hope*?

_____

_____

_____

_____

_____

_____

_____

_____

_____

_____

_____

_____

_____

_____

_____

_____

_____

_____

_____

_____

_____

_____

_____

_____

_____

Day 175

find a local *Clothing Organization* that will pick up slightly used clothes, gather your slightly used clothes and *schedule a pickup*, usually they provide curbside pickup. Help the less fortunate in your community you may never see.

Day 176

Look up *five new words* and write the definition from the dictionary and rewrite in your words.

Can't:

isn't a description applied to a uncompleted action or unfulfilled quest... it is more self-made barricade than sledgehammer, some walls require the deconstructive approach... either knock it down, break through it, or find the most efficient route around it. Choose the best option available and keep moving.

Day 177

Write a Poem:
and You Are The *Only One* Who Knows

Day 178

Art Appreciation Day: Locate your local ***Museum of Art.*** Wear comfortable shoes and take a group to view the art or go by yourself, take your time. ***Read the titles*** and the ***name of the artist,*** pay attention to details. If a picture is worth a thousand words, return to writing and write words worth a thousand pictures.

Day 179

A Lesson In Metaphors: Describe ***The Process*** of Driving A Car From ***Point A*** to ***Point B***, without using the word ***Car*** and begin writing the process ***before you get inside*** of the Vehicle…

_____

_____

_____

_____

_____

_____

_____

_____

_____

_____

_____

_____

_____

_____

_____

_____

_____

_____

_____

_____

_____

_____

_____

_____

_____

_____

_____

_____

Day 180

Day 181

Take a friend, your children, a lover or a group to the *'Movies Night'*, you can agree on what to see before you leave or *surprise yourself* with a *newly released* movie starring your favorite movie star or an actor / actress you kind of like. *It's Movie Night*. Purchase a bag of popcorn and a drink too.

Day 182

And Used My Heart *As Bait*

Day 183

Write a song of struggle, not of sadness for struggling... ***of pain*** but not of the hurt pain brings, but the knowledge received from going through the process.

Day 184

Write a *Short Story* About Your Childhood

_____

_____

_____

_____

_____

_____

_____

_____

_____

_____

_____

_____

_____

_____

_____

_____

_____

_____

_____

_____

_____

_____

_____

_____

_____

Day 185

We often use *All* and *Love* in the same sentence, *write your definition of All...*

_____

_____

_____

_____

_____

_____

_____

_____

_____

_____

_____

_____

_____

_____

_____

_____

_____

_____

_____

_____

_____

_____

_____

Day 186

Write a Poem to Your First Born Child (or The Poem You Will Read *When* You Have A Child)

Day 187

What happens when Love goes unsaid? When we quiet our tongues in ***fear of rejection***? When we only admire from ***eyes distance*** and smile close up? Explain: ***Undiscovered Love***

_____

_____

_____

_____

_____

_____

_____

_____

_____

_____

_____

_____

_____

_____

_____

_____

_____

_____

_____

_____

_____

_____

_____

Day 188

Write A Short Story of *Your Favorite Fad* you enjoyed during your *Youth*, ie... *Bellbottoms*, Punk Rock, Big Hair, *Hip Hop Styles*, Jerry Curl, *Suede Shoes*, Bebop, Boy Bands, *Girl Bands*... *etc*...

Day 189

Find the nearest **Homeless Shelter** in your community. Today, visit the homeless shelter, most are in need of toiletries and other daily necessities. Today your visit is to familiarize yourself with what is needed to see what you can do to help. Make it *your mission* once a month.

Day 190

For your play: Congratulations you have just completed writing dialogue, one or two scenes and at least
one act. *The dialogue* and scenes are the foundation of
any great stage play. If the dialogue does not speak to
the audience and the scene does not serve as medium
through which the dialogue is clearly conveyed to an
audience, your stage play does not have a strong
enough base to stand on. *Take a moment* to go over
what you have written so far...

Day 191

Truth is: we *live to die* or we are *dying to live*… however you choose to say it - our stay here is not a permanent one, we are only allowed a visit to fulfill the mission appointed us *before we knew* we were breathers… Tell me of *your mission* or describe to me *your Purpose*

Day 192

Define Amazing In Your Own Words

Day 193   Write a *Short Story* About Your *Years* In High School

Day 194

Write a letter to the person you know, who had *faith in you* and challenged you to want to do better. Tell them the *words or actions* used that enabled you *to believe* in you too.

Day 195

Write a *Poem or Short Story* of *Your Favorite Season.* *Explain Why* It Is Your Favorite...

Day 196

for your movie... Write a chance meeting of the main character and adversary, have them glance at each other in passing or a meeting of chance attending the same event, or give each one a quick glance at the other as though they were but were not paying attention to what the other one was doing..

Day 197 *Five Things* I Keep In My *Pocket or Purse*, and why

_____

_____

_____

_____

_____

_____

_____

_____

_____

_____

_____

_____

_____

_____

_____

_____

_____

_____

_____

_____

_____

_____

_____

_____

_____

_____

_____

_____

Day 198

Write a *Love Poem* to *Your Purpose*

_____
_____
_____
_____
_____
_____
_____
_____
_____
_____
_____
_____
_____
_____
_____
_____
_____
_____
_____
_____
_____
_____
_____
_____
_____
_____
_____

Day 199

Describe The *Sound of Struggle*

_____
_____
_____
_____
_____
_____
_____
_____
_____
_____
_____
_____
_____
_____
_____
_____
_____
_____
_____
_____
_____
_____
_____
_____
_____
_____
_____
_____
_____
_____

Day 200

Write a Short *Story of winter*, with cold being a creature, and snow a monster. Describe winter as a place

Day 201

Lessons from *My Childhood*

_____

_____

_____

_____

_____

_____

_____

_____

_____

_____

_____

_____

_____

_____

_____

_____

_____

_____

_____

_____

_____

_____

_____

_____

_____

_____

_____

_____

_____

_____

_____

_____

Day 202

Look up *five new words* and write the definition from the dictionary and rewrite in your words.

_____

_____

_____

_____

_____

_____

_____

_____

_____

_____

_____

_____

_____

_____

_____

_____

_____

_____

_____

_____

_____

_____

_____

_____

Day 203   Write a *Short Story* About Your *Years in College*

_____

_____

_____

_____

_____

_____

_____

_____

_____

_____

_____

_____

_____

_____

_____

_____

_____

_____

_____

_____

_____

_____

_____

_____

_____

_____

_____

_____

_____

_____

_____

_____

Day 204

Design a Quilt using the Gifts given you by All of the People who have Supported You In Your Life's Journey So Far... give each *Patch a Color...* Explain what each Color means.

_____
_____
_____
_____
_____
_____
_____
_____
_____
_____
_____
_____
_____
_____
_____
_____
_____
_____
_____
_____
_____
_____
_____
_____
_____
_____
_____
_____

Day 205

Define *in your words* Forever.

_____

_____

_____

_____

_____

_____

_____

_____

_____

_____

_____

_____

_____

_____

_____

_____

_____

_____

_____

_____

_____

_____

_____

_____

_____

_____

Every so often

you must be the one

to congratulate you

be your biggest supporter

cheering squad

wing man or woman

flag bearer

drummer

and

drum roll provider

cake baker

Professional Pyrotechnician

the conductor of your personal

orchestra or band

the last one

will be determined

by your choice of music

Day 206

Write an outline for the dialog between your main character and sidekick, for your ***Children's Book or Fairytale*** after solving the first obstacle or problem. Use at least two different methods attempted before actually agreeing. Give the sidekick a major role in coming up with the solution.

Day 207

Explain Why: This Is The Season For *Living / Life*

_____

_____

_____

_____

_____

_____

_____

_____

_____

_____

_____

_____

_____

_____

_____

_____

_____

_____

_____

_____

_____

_____

_____

_____

_____

Day 208

This Is The *Last Time* I..

Day 209

If Love stories are the in thing. Write a Short Story: *The Story of We…*

Day 210

There are many *Mentoring Organizations* across the nation, most are nonprofit. *Check your area* to see what services they perform and if there are ways to support monetarily. Usually a *minimal donation* is $5 - $10 dollars. Donate what you can, *a little* goes a long way.

Day 211

Define Faith...

_____

_____

_____

_____

_____

_____

_____

_____

_____

_____

_____

_____

_____

_____

_____

_____

_____

_____

_____

_____

_____

_____

_____

_____

_____

Day 212

When it comes to discovery, life has always offered us *choices*... here is a list of all the Places *I Will Never Forget*

_____

_____

_____

_____

_____

_____

_____

_____

_____

_____

_____

_____

_____

_____

_____

_____

_____

_____

_____

_____

_____

_____

_____

_____

_____

_____

_____

Day 213

Day 214

Day 215

What lessons can you learn, and are our emotions expressed louder *In Silence: give examples.* Explain

_____

_____

_____

_____

_____

_____

_____

_____

_____

_____

_____

_____

_____

_____

_____

_____

_____

_____

_____

_____

_____

_____

_____

_____

_____

_____

_____

_____

_____

_____

_____

Day 216

What *Title* Would You *Give Yourself?* (CEO, Author, Poet, Rapper, Dancer, Painter, Teacher, Motivator...) *Explain* Why You *Wear It* Proudly...

_____

_____

_____

_____

_____

_____

_____

_____

_____

_____

_____

_____

_____

_____

_____

_____

_____

_____

_____

_____

_____

_____

_____

_____

_____

_____

_____

Day 217

For your play: after reviewing, does it say or read as you thought when you were writing it? Does each character *possess* their own unique voice? In your mind does the scenes move into place? What is *the reason* for the play? Does the characters move toward *creating an incident*? or solving a problem you've presented, is there *an event* they are attending? *Make the purpose* of their interactions and dialog present *within the script* and movement of the actors.

Day 218

Write *Yourself* an Apology

_____

_____

_____

_____

_____

_____

_____

_____

_____

_____

_____

_____

_____

_____

_____

_____

_____

_____

_____

_____

_____

_____

_____

_____

_____

_____

_____

_____

_____

_____

Day 219

There are always *new stage plays* presented in your area, some starring *local actors* and other plays receiving national acclaim. *Find a local stage play* to see, stay around, talk with the *director and the actors,* you may love it and decide to come back.

Day 220

Write a Short Story of *a day in the life* of the *child* you used to be. Write of fun, the games you played *outside*, or in the park, play ground or in the street. You can add the *nicknames* of the friends who joined you in the activities.

Day 221

15 Reasons Why I Miss You...

Day 222

The Importance of *Keeping Secrets* or *Not Having* Them At All...

Day 223

A Time or *A Call* to Action

Day 224

for your movie... describe the complete scene of the first *open confrontation*, are they alone or in a crowed space, *where* does it take place, will this be the only one or will there be some way it is interrupted before the climax? Write it out.

_____

_____

_____

_____

_____

_____

_____

_____

_____

_____

_____

_____

_____

_____

_____

_____

_____

_____

_____

_____

_____

_____

_____

_____

_____

Day 225

Day 226

A Lesson in imagery: stand in front of a mirror, pen and paper in hand. Write *10 descriptive* lines, each one painting an image of how you see yourself close up, ie... blemishes, beauty marks, *scars*, the shape and *color* of your eyes, lips, smile, nose, ears, *etc...*

Day 227

_____ Gets *Lost In* The Journey, explain

Day 228

There Are *Generations* Waiting

Day 229

The organization *Big Brother Big Sister* are always in need of people to become a mentor. Find the local chapter and sign up to participate once a month.

Day 230

Look up *five new words* and write the definition from the dictionary and rewrite in your words.

_____

_____

_____

_____

_____

_____

_____

_____

_____

_____

_____

_____

_____

_____

_____

_____

_____

_____

_____

_____

_____

_____

_____

_____

_____

_____

_____

_____

Day 231

Deep In The *Corner of* Your Smile

Day 232

Where I Came From

_____

Day 233

What Is *Free* or *Define* Freedom

Day 234

On *The Other* Side of Town

_____

_____

_____

_____

_____

_____

_____

_____

_____

_____

_____

_____

_____

_____

_____

_____

_____

_____

_____

_____

_____

_____

_____

_____

_____

_____

_____

_____

_____

_____

_____

Dreaming while in slumber and day dreaming are not the same thing... the first: you may or may not remember the circumstances under which the thought came to mind, the other: you have the opportunity to write it down, build on it, and bring it to fruition. We should all prefer the latter, but make sure you add enough follow through to make it happen.

Day 235

For your Children's Book or Fairytale *describe at least two scenes* for the first portion of *their adventure.* ie... rain forest, desert, city, alleyway, basement of a high rise... *use your imagination.*

Day 236

If *music* is your thing this will be quite enlightening. If it is not your thing it will be very exhilarating... *locate the venue* in your area where a local band will be performing, *dress* for the occasion and get there early. Enjoy the *new songs* you may hear on the radio soon. We will call this *'Discover the Talent Around You Day'*.

Day 237

For you play: Review the ***Plot***…The Plot must advance *(move along with)* with the characters and the dialog… ***grow your story***, if a character can do instead of say, let the audience see it, ***clearly define the role*** of each actor in your stage play, ***their voice***, the way they move, their interactions… ***let each character own*** their ***piece of stage*** they are standing on.

Day 238

What are *3 Things* You would Tell the *One* You Love Every Morning and repeat *every day* as the Sun sets

Day 239

Describe The *Steps In Order* to Accomplish A Specific Task or Mission...*Explain each* Component of the Process and *What the Task* or *Mission is...*

_____

_____

_____

_____

_____

_____

_____

_____

_____

_____

_____

_____

_____

_____

_____

_____

_____

_____

_____

_____

_____

_____

_____

_____

_____

_____

_____

_____

_____

Day 240

Carrying *yesterday's* wrapped tightly in cellophane, will not enable you to tread through your *tomorrows* lightly, it only means you've brought too much luggage to participate in this track meet towards Destiny. *How will you lighten your load?*

Day 241

What I Know About Segregation

Day 242

My *Grandmother* Always Said

Day 243

In working on your movie… list the actors and actresses you like, *make a list* of movies you adore, include all types. Study the things you liked about them. Notice the relationships, the scenery, the scenes, the cuts, fades and transitions. *Most of all,* the scripting of the dialog. Compare your writings on your movie to *what you loved* about others and see how it adds up.

Day 244

A Piece *Of Fire* In The Rain

Day 245

Write a ***Short Story of an Addiction.*** It doesn't have to be ***drugs***… there are a lot of things we do if you look closer we have created addictions out of them. Cell Phone, Internet Sites, Fast Food, Shopping… ***pick one*** or use the one you have created for ***yourself.***

Day 246

There is so *Much More* to Say

Day 247

Every *Time I Look* Back

Day 248

There are *organizations* you don't have to be a member of *to donate* or help, when performing acts within the community. *Become an active member* in the betterment of the area around you. Some activities are *seasonal,* some are *monthly* and some *once a year*. Choose one and *sign up*.

_____
_____
_____
_____
_____
_____
_____
_____
_____
_____
_____
_____
_____
_____
_____
_____
_____
_____
_____
_____
_____
_____
_____
_____
_____
_____
_____
_____

Day 249

Can *Complaining Be Effective* as a *Solution* to any Possible Problem: Yes or No… *Discuss*

_____

_____

_____

_____

_____

_____

_____

_____

_____

_____

_____

_____

_____

_____

_____

_____

_____

_____

_____

_____

_____

_____

_____

_____

_____

_____

_____

_____

_____

Day 250

Although *Un Noticed* The Flag *Waves On*

Day 251

for your movie… write in *separate paragraphs* how each of the main characters in the story are preparing for the *next* chance meeting. What *skills* or *techniques* will be required for the winner. Does either one of them need *a teacher* or *private instructor*, or does one of them already possess the needed skills to defeat the other? *Write it out*

Day 252

Day 253

If My Feet *Were Wheels* or *Wings*

_____

_____

_____

_____

_____

_____

_____

_____

_____

_____

_____

_____

_____

_____

_____

_____

_____

_____

_____

_____

_____

_____

_____

_____

_____

_____

_____

_____

_____

_____

Day 254

We *believe* in fate or *say accidents happen*, if most of the *greatest inventions* were created while attempting to solve a different problem or equation... *would that* somehow mean *Randomness* is an associate of perfection? *Explain Randomness* as a form of art.

Day 255

During *summer,* local recreation centers have many various *youth activities* during the day and early evenings, find a recreation center near you, see what *role* you can fill to help with any of the *ongoing programs*; if not, *see about starting a program* of your own you would like to share. There is *always room* for more help.

Day 256

Why Aren't *Relationships* Perfect?

Day 257

Look up *five new words* and write the definition from the dictionary and rewrite in your words.

_____

_____

_____

_____

_____

_____

_____

_____

_____

_____

_____

_____

_____

_____

_____

_____

_____

_____

_____

_____

_____

_____

_____

_____

_____

_____

_____

_____

Day 258

Day 259

There Is *One Thing* I Know For Sure

Day 260

Create Your *Personal Success Map*... Start at *You Are Here* and *Diagram or Graph* each Stage, Step or Route You Must Take To Attain *Your Desired* Outcome

_____

_____

_____

_____

_____

_____

_____

_____

_____

_____

_____

_____

_____

_____

_____

_____

_____

_____

_____

_____

_____

_____

_____

_____

_____

_____

_____

Day 261

Write A *Love Song* to the Person *You Love*

_____

_____

_____

_____

_____

_____

_____

_____

_____

_____

_____

_____

_____

_____

_____

_____

_____

_____

_____

_____

_____

_____

_____

_____

_____

_____

_____

_____

_____

_____

Day 262

Design a new dance: Write the directions for the steps… include the fronts, backs and side to sides. To begin, **choose the type of music** you will create the dance for, fast, slow or calypso.

Day 263

as summer comes *to an end*, support a *local event* or a *drive for school supplies* and other items students require to have a successful year. Locate an organization participating in *furnishing supplies* for youth in your community, or purchase paper, pens, crayons, *backpacks* or any of the items on the list and donate.

_____

_____

_____

_____

_____

_____

_____

_____

_____

_____

_____

_____

_____

_____

_____

_____

_____

_____

_____

_____

_____

_____

_____

_____

_____

Day 264

for your Children's Book or Fairytale: *write the meeting or confrontation between your villain*, main character and sidekick... *describe* it in a way there are multiple options of solving, or not solving the problem or obstacle.

_____

_____

_____

_____

_____

_____

_____

_____

_____

_____

_____

_____

_____

_____

_____

_____

_____

_____

_____

_____

_____

_____

_____

_____

_____

_____

_____

_____

Day 265

Write A Short Story:
The Story *of When* We First Started...

_____

_____

_____

_____

_____

_____

_____

_____

_____

_____

_____

_____

_____

_____

_____

_____

_____

_____

_____

_____

_____

_____

_____

_____

_____

_____

_____

_____

_____

If you think telling others what you are working on, or creating, will garner their support, think again... most will attempt to discourage you - or claim it is impossible and to make it sound authentic - they will add names of people they know or read about who failed to accomplish something similar... prepare your response in advance... let them know - "impossible was a term used or a mythical creature created in the era of dragons and flat earth, it was destroyed either in the ice age with the dinosaurs, or burned at the stake in the Salem... to date, no one has found any of its fragments, or discovered where the remains are buried". Then hurriedly get back to work... time is of the essence.

Day 266

The Shadows of My Past

_____

_____

_____

_____

_____

_____

_____

_____

_____

_____

_____

_____

_____

_____

_____

_____

_____

_____

_____

_____

_____

_____

_____

_____

_____

_____

_____

_____

_____

_____

Day 267

Describe the *Difference* between *Civil Rights* and *Civil Liberties*... from the human perspective

_____
_____
_____
_____
_____
_____
_____
_____
_____
_____
_____
_____
_____
_____
_____
_____
_____
_____
_____
_____
_____
_____
_____
_____
_____

Name a fictional Place _____, create a name for a mountain _____, (this mountain was so tall if it wasn't destroyed, the earth would be thrown out of balance). Create an Ancient

Day 268

Race _____. Write you a Legend… using the three items you've created. Tell the story "In the Days before Myths". Think of all the Greeks gods and how those stories were told, now… Write, the Legend of You: replace the You with the name of the Race you created.

_____

_____

_____

_____

_____

_____

_____

_____

_____

_____

_____

_____

_____

_____

_____

_____

_____

_____

_____

_____

_____

_____

_____

_____

_____

Day 269

I Love You *Because*...

Day 270

This Time *Next Year*

_____

_____

_____

_____

_____

_____

_____

_____

_____

_____

_____

_____

_____

_____

_____

_____

_____

_____

_____

_____

_____

_____

_____

_____

_____

_____

_____

_____

_____

Day 271

Day 272

Describe the moon, include the ***shapes,*** how long it takes ***to change***, where it goes ***to hide*** from the sun, and do not use the word ***moon*** at all in your description.

_____

_____

_____

_____

_____

_____

_____

_____

_____

_____

_____

_____

_____

_____

_____

_____

_____

_____

_____

_____

_____

_____

_____

_____

_____

_____

_____

_____

Day 273

Day 274

Often I *Find Myself* Broken

_____

_____

_____

_____

_____

_____

_____

_____

_____

_____

_____

_____

_____

_____

_____

_____

_____

_____

_____

_____

_____

_____

_____

_____

_____

_____

_____

_____

_____

_____

_____

_____

Day 275

Today take a *friend*, family member or *loved one* to the *local park*, put on your *comfortable shoes*, prepare a snack or lunch if need be... do not be in a *rush* today, *slow down* and view nature as it was meant to be seen. *Spend an evening in the Park.*

_____

_____

_____

_____

_____

_____

_____

_____

_____

_____

_____

_____

_____

_____

_____

_____

_____

_____

_____

_____

_____

_____

_____

_____

_____

_____

_____

_____

Day 276

My First Best Friend...

_____
_____
_____
_____
_____
_____
_____
_____
_____
_____
_____
_____
_____
_____
_____
_____
_____
_____
_____
_____
_____
_____
_____
_____
_____
_____
_____
_____
_____
_____
_____
_____

Day 277 This Is *the Last Time*, I will *Share* All Of *Me* With You

Day 278

Describe the *Sound of Laughter* (without using the word *Laugh*)

_____

_____

_____

_____

_____

_____

_____

_____

_____

_____

_____

_____

_____

_____

_____

_____

_____

_____

_____

_____

_____

_____

_____

_____

_____

_____

_____

_____

_____

_____

Day 279

It is easy to hide in the light of day, but *When Night Falls...* Explain *the battle of Thinking,* or the *war* between your thoughts when alone.

Day 280

Write a short story *encouraging* someone *(use a name)* to *keep fighting*, create a *real life* problem / obstacle, and detail *both sides* of the conversation.

_____

_____

_____

_____

_____

_____

_____

_____

_____

_____

_____

_____

_____

_____

_____

_____

_____

_____

_____

_____

_____

_____

_____

_____

_____

_____

_____

_____

Day 281

This Is My *Second Time* Here

Day 282

Write a Eulogy or the Eulogy you would like read when the ***time arrives...*** include the ***failures***, accomplishments and a few things ***you regret*** the occurrence of.

_____

_____

_____

_____

_____

_____

_____

_____

_____

_____

_____

_____

_____

_____

_____

_____

_____

_____

_____

_____

_____

_____

_____

_____

_____

_____

_____

_____

Day 283

for your movie... is there a *damsel in distress*, a world *under siege*, a city about to be *destroyed*, a family in *danger*? Whatever the situation is you are building to a climatic end bring it to the *forefront* in this scene., make it as *detailed* and as *graphic* as your imagination will allow.

Day 284

For The Purpose of This Prompt *You Are a Farmer:*
If *Knowledge* Was Water and Your Children Were
Seeds... Describe Your Unique *Process* of Farming

Day 285

Look up *five new words* and write the definition from the dictionary and rewrite in your words.

_____

_____

_____

_____

_____

_____

_____

_____

_____

_____

_____

_____

_____

_____

_____

_____

_____

_____

_____

_____

_____

_____

_____

_____

_____

_____

_____

_____

Day 286

Come *Judgment Day*

Day 287

A Lesson in Metaphor: Write The *Detailed* Process and Experience of *Riding A Roller* Coaster (*without* using the word Roller Coaster)

Day 288

Most downtown areas have a ***soup kitchen*** or something similar. Locate the ***one in your city*** and volunteer ***once a month.*** Call or use whatever method of ***contacting*** them you prefer and inquire what is needed to ***participate*** or what you could do to ***help*** in some way.

_____

_____

_____

_____

_____

_____

_____

_____

_____

_____

_____

_____

_____

_____

_____

_____

_____

_____

_____

_____

_____

_____

_____

_____

_____

_____

_____

Day 289

Describe the *Road to Change*, and *explain* what you are changing.

_____

_____

_____

_____

_____

_____

_____

_____

_____

_____

_____

_____

_____

_____

_____

_____

_____

_____

_____

_____

_____

_____

_____

_____

_____

Day 290

When I *Think of Fun* I Think Of...

_____

_____

_____

_____

_____

_____

_____

_____

_____

_____

_____

_____

_____

_____

_____

_____

_____

_____

_____

_____

_____

_____

_____

_____

_____

_____

_____

Day 291

re introduce the *sub characters into the storyline for your children's book or fairytale*: detail the group discussion on *how to approach* the solution to the problem or obstacle you've created for them.

_____

_____

_____

_____

_____

_____

_____

_____

_____

_____

_____

_____

_____

_____

_____

_____

_____

_____

_____

_____

_____

_____

_____

_____

_____

_____

_____

_____

_____

_____

_____

Day 292

Describe the Sound of a body of *water*. ie...
Lake / Sea / River / Ocean

_____
_____
_____
_____
_____
_____
_____
_____
_____
_____
_____
_____
_____
_____
_____
_____
_____
_____
_____
_____
_____
_____
_____
_____
_____
_____
_____
_____

Day 293

_____ Drives Me *Crazy, explain*

Day 294

Write *a morning note* to someone *you love* to slip in their *pocket or purse* as a surprise…

_____

_____

_____

_____

_____

_____

_____

_____

_____

_____

_____

_____

_____

_____

_____

_____

_____

_____

_____

_____

_____

_____

_____

_____

_____

_____

_____

_____

Day 295

A Prompt for *Framing:* Take your *age*, divide it by *three*, pay no attention to the decimal, you now have three numbers, write them down, we will label them *Cycles*, (only for this prompt)... *Write a Letter* or *Poem* to your *mother*; thanking her, *using specifics* in each cycle of your life. Possible titles *"Cycles of Time"*, "Three Life Cycles" or "Cycles".

Day 296

Buy a Book written by an ***Unknown*** or ***Local Author,*** Read It and ***Post*** Your Comments on The Site, where you purchased it …

Stop

erasing

what you write

some days

your pen

is much smarter

than you

will ever be

Day 297

When *Your Hands* Are Tied

_____

_____

_____

_____

_____

_____

_____

_____

_____

_____

_____

_____

_____

_____

_____

_____

_____

_____

_____

_____

_____

_____

_____

_____

_____

_____

_____

_____

_____

_____

_____

_____

Day 298

Write a Short Story: of a programmable *ink pen* you could give instructions to write a story… only *today* the ink pen *malfunctioned*; and began writing its own story, at least you **thought it was** until you begin to read the words, and found it was writing *all the secrets* it *knew* about you.

Day 299

Tonight Take the Person That *Means Everything* to You *outside* and Write Your Names Using the Stars as Alphabets

Day 300

for your movie... write at least *three possible* outcomes or scenarios for the *last scene*, place in this scene as many ways to *fail* as you create to solve the problem or situation. This should be your *most descriptive* and imaginative challenge to *keep the viewer* or reader wondering, which *direction* you will take it.

Day 301

Fear Is...

_____

_____

_____

_____

_____

_____

_____

_____

_____

_____

_____

_____

_____

_____

_____

_____

_____

_____

_____

_____

_____

_____

_____

_____

_____

_____

_____

_____

_____

_____

Day 302

Write a letter of encouragement to *someone* who encouraged you who *may have* lost their way.

Day 303

Define: Restore or Restoration

Day 304

It's **Breakfast Day**. Locate a local establishment you haven't ventured to, that serves **breakfast** and enjoy the food with **friends and family** or be the first to try it. Supporting **local businesses** has to be a part of our community service. **Write about the experience**

Day 305

put on *your best smile*, we are donating smiles. Pick at least *five houses* on the street or apartments in the building in which you live, go *introduce yourself.* Practice what you will say before embarking on a mission of *meet and greet.* Write the names and numbers (*door or address*) on this page to help you *remember.*

Day 306

For You I Would...
do not include the *impossibles's,* make a list of
all the things you have *done and will do* for Love.

_____
_____
_____
_____
_____
_____
_____
_____
_____
_____
_____
_____
_____
_____
_____
_____
_____
_____
_____
_____
_____
_____
_____
_____
_____
_____
_____
_____
_____

Day 307

What was *your favorite dish* or meal *growing up*? Who prepared it? Without help, *write the ingredients* and cooking instructions if you were to *fix it*

_____

_____

_____

_____

_____

_____

_____

_____

_____

_____

_____

_____

_____

_____

_____

_____

_____

_____

_____

_____

_____

_____

_____

_____

_____

_____

Day 308

Write a Short Story of the stories your *favorite pair* of shoes would tell *if ever* they were asked where they have been?

Day 309

For Your Play: make sure you have dressed the actions and appeal of *each character* well, so everyone who auditions would like to play every *attractive role* you've created. Give each character *a moment* in the sun that would appear to *highlight* their abilities to enable them shine in the lights. *Write it in the script,* let each character *at some point* give the impression they are in *control*.

Day 310

Write a Short Story about the *manufacturing* process of a *smart television* able to have full conversations with the people *watching* … make it *very intolerant* and *opinionated*, it only likes specific *programs* (list the programs), and once it is installed in your house it *cannot* be removed.

Day 311

The Very *First Time*

Day 312

Write a Love Poem ... do not include sex or sex acts, a poem *of emotions*, of time spent, of movement, *of togetherness*. You can make it a song by *writing a hook*, chorus or refrain to be added later.

_____

_____

_____

_____

_____

_____

_____

_____

_____

_____

_____

_____

_____

_____

_____

_____

_____

_____

_____

_____

_____

_____

_____

_____

_____

_____

_____

_____

_____

Day 313

I Discovered _____ in The Sunrise
Tell the whole story...

_____
_____
_____
_____
_____
_____
_____
_____
_____
_____
_____
_____
_____
_____
_____
_____
_____
_____
_____
_____
_____
_____
_____
_____
_____
_____
_____
_____

Day 314

Write a note to yourself to summon a positive reaction each time you read it. Make a list of the things you *wish* to attain or *complete*, beside each item, place the *action* needed by you to complete it.

_____

_____

_____

_____

_____

_____

_____

_____

_____

_____

_____

_____

_____

_____

_____

_____

_____

_____

_____

_____

_____

_____

_____

_____

Day 315

Look up *five new words* and write the definition from the dictionary and rewrite in your words.

_____

_____

_____

_____

_____

_____

_____

_____

_____

_____

_____

_____

_____

_____

_____

_____

_____

_____

_____

_____

_____

_____

_____

_____

_____

_____

_____

Day 316

We all have *family members* or friends that are *battling a deadly disease,* pick one of the organizations that are doing a *5k walk or run*, a river walk, or *a rally* to raise money and *awareness* for a cure… either sign up to walk, run, or *donate* to the cause.

Day 317

Write a song *of rest, or a lullaby* to sing to a *baby*.

Day 318

Neighborhood / Community Exploration Day, make today a *slow fun* day, take a drive through your community *use* the streets you seldom or never travel, you may discover *a route* to take to get to a place you always have to go. There are *ways* to learn something new every day. *Explore.*

_____

Day 319

We lose our keys, ***our jackets***, our cell phones, some say ***our minds***... if you per chance went ***Searching For Yesterday,*** what would you be looking for?

Day 320

If Hearts *could Talk or Speak*, would yours *echo* the same sentiments *you use* to express the words you say to those you say you have *feelings* for? or would you have to *find* ways to keep it quiet? *Explain*

Day 321

detail each step, including one failed try... for the characters in your Children's Book or Fairytale, before ***they arrive*** at the ***method used*** to solve the first problem or obstacle.

_____

_____

_____

_____

_____

_____

_____

_____

_____

_____

_____

_____

_____

_____

_____

_____

_____

_____

_____

_____

_____

_____

_____

_____

_____

_____

_____

_____

_____

Day 322

_____
_____
_____
_____
_____
_____
_____
_____
_____
_____
_____
_____
_____
_____
_____
_____
_____
_____
_____
_____
_____
_____
_____
_____
_____
_____
_____
_____
_____
_____

Day 323

We have all had ***best friends*** we are ***no longer best*** with. ***Write the letter*** you have written a thousand times in ***your mind*** to get your best friend back. It may include ***a couple*** of my faults, ***I'm sorry's***, and forgive me's, ***write it*** as though you plan to hand deliver it ***to the person*** in question.

_____

_____

_____

_____

_____

_____

_____

_____

_____

_____

_____

_____

_____

_____

_____

_____

_____

_____

_____

_____

_____

_____

_____

Day 324

Write 4 each *Haiku's*, using (Irony)

Day 325

We all *possess an inner power*, some say it is a *voice*, others say it's our *higher conscience*... what do you *believe* it is? and how would you *explain* the process?

_____

_____

_____

_____

_____

_____

_____

_____

_____

_____

_____

_____

_____

_____

_____

_____

_____

_____

_____

_____

_____

_____

_____

_____

Day 326

If and When

Day 327

The phrase Me, Myself and I has always been a popular one to describe conversations or time spent with self... *Write* a Short Story entailing the plight of *Me, Myself and We...*

_____

_____

_____

_____

_____

_____

_____

_____

_____

_____

_____

_____

_____

_____

_____

_____

_____

_____

_____

_____

_____

_____

_____

_____

_____

_____

_____

_____

_____

rising from the ashes

only means

you possess the DNA

of a mythical Phoenix

your thoughts are rejuvenated

on the hour, every hour

watch the clock if you must

giving up

has never been a choice

you could make

nor was it written

in your life's diary

for you to check off

as an option

Day 328

I Found the *Best Me* through the *Fog*

Day 329

Write an *Angry Poem*, and treat anger as a treatable *disease* you can receive *prescription's* for: *and I Stopped Taking My Meds This Morning*

Day 330

What is the *title* of the last book you read *that held your attention* so close you couldn't put it down until you finished reading? Give the *title and Author*. Now, what aspects of *that book* would you like to see in other books you read, *mainly* in the book you are writing?

_____

_____

_____

_____

_____

_____

_____

_____

_____

_____

_____

_____

_____

_____

_____

_____

_____

_____

_____

_____

_____

_____

_____

_____

_____

Day 331

for your movie... is this a movie where the *villain* or *adversary* comes out victorious or the *main character* comes out the victor by an *unforeseen* participant, or the *introduction* of a new character *leaving room* for a *sequel*? Think it through...then *write it* out.

Day 332

This year *participate* in the *Aids Walk* for a Cure, usually it is *5k or 10k,* the more people aware of this disease *will prevent* others from getting it or passing it on. *Sign up* and join the fight.

_____

_____

_____

_____

_____

_____

_____

_____

_____

_____

_____

_____

_____

_____

_____

_____

_____

_____

_____

_____

_____

_____

_____

_____

_____

Day 333

Write a Poem in the form of *Alliteration.*

_____
_____
_____
_____
_____
_____
_____
_____
_____
_____
_____
_____
_____
_____
_____
_____
_____
_____
_____
_____
_____
_____
_____
_____
_____

Day 334

Write the conversation you have with your computer, cell phone or I-pad... I catch myself talking to mine often, so I know we have them. ***Write*** your conversation and the ***why of it***.

Day 335

Write or Create *7 Steps* for Building *Character*

_____

_____

_____

_____

_____

_____

_____

_____

_____

_____

_____

_____

_____

_____

_____

_____

_____

_____

_____

_____

_____

_____

_____

_____

_____

_____

_____

Day 336

In the Marrow of *My Bones*

Day 337

Make *a list of the differences* between a friend and an associate, it seems today *the lines* have become blurred making it *hard to tell* which is which. Draw a line down the center of the page, *one side* friend the other side associate.

Day 338

Write a Poem to your child before he or she *graduates* high school, *explaining* what's to come, and *how to* maintain their conscious while exploring *life without borders.* Congratulate them on making it this far, add some *I love you's*, I am proud of you's... end it with a *warning* about how real life can be when you are *your choices*.

_____

_____

_____

_____

_____

_____

_____

_____

_____

_____

_____

_____

_____

_____

_____

_____

_____

_____

_____

_____

_____

_____

Day 339

Today hope you were *observant... write a description* of your transit to work or on your hustle... include the *people* you passed, or accompanied you on the train, bus or plane. *Write* a Short Story or poem about *getting there.*

_____
_____
_____
_____
_____
_____
_____
_____
_____
_____
_____
_____
_____
_____
_____
_____
_____
_____
_____
_____
_____
_____
_____
_____
_____
_____

Day 340

For Your Play: You have reviewed the script, refined the *dialog,* added distinctive *tones and voices*, replaced the words that can be displayed by *movement*, insured each role has the moment *center stage*. I must say *congratulations* again for making it here, on the precipice of *completion*. Review, reread, restructure and double check. *You are ready to put it all together.*

Day 341

Write *10 ways of discovering* or detecting *Doubt...*
Doubt appears using different names and often in
disguise, ie... any means or method used to slow or
stop *your progress*.

Day 342

In every relationship, sometimes the **smallest** issues appear larger when ***left silent***. Write a ***Short Story*** of one of your real life issues you haven't discussed or ***gotten over***. Change the names please.. ***it is just a story.***

_____

_____

_____

_____

_____

_____

_____

_____

_____

_____

_____

_____

_____

_____

_____

_____

_____

_____

_____

_____

_____

_____

_____

_____

_____

_____

_____

_____

Day 343

Maybe It Was *Yesterday*

Day 344

Help a neighbor in your community. Waving is the usual **greeting** with no words being passed. Today **look for ways** to help someone, **anyone** in your community that may be in need of **help**. It will often consist of something **simple** that will only require **minutes** of your time.

_____

_____
_____
_____
_____
_____
_____
_____
_____
_____
_____
_____
_____
_____
_____
_____
_____
_____
_____
_____
_____
_____
_____
_____
_____
_____
_____
_____

Day 345

Look up *five new words* and write the definition from the dictionary and rewrite in your words.

Day 346

After All...

_____

Day 347

It is said *Patience is a Virtue*... How do you locate your center for *Patience* or how do you gain *more* Patience?

_____

_____

_____

_____

_____

_____

_____

_____

_____

_____

_____

_____

_____

_____

_____

_____

_____

_____

_____

_____

_____

_____

_____

_____

Day 348

When it comes to *Purpose and Destiny* what is the difference between *Wait and Weight*? Explain…

Day 349

How *Much Truth* is Enough Truth?
How *Much Truth* Can You Take?

Day 350

describe a brief celebration for the characters in your Children's Book or Fairytale, *after solving* the first problem or obstacle.

_____

_____

_____

_____

_____

_____

_____

_____

_____

_____

_____

_____

_____

_____

_____

_____

_____

_____

_____

_____

_____

_____

_____

_____

_____

Day 351

Do you remember how *innocence* felt? Write a Short Story of *Innocence Lost* and how.

Day 352

Write a Poem: *If You Were here*

_____
_____
_____
_____
_____
_____
_____
_____
_____
_____
_____
_____
_____
_____
_____
_____
_____
_____
_____
_____
_____
_____
_____
_____
_____
_____
_____
_____
_____

Day 353

Write a Short Story detailing *a Super Power you received*, explain how you *received it*, and what it is, how you use it. Within the story tell if you would use it to have a *positive effect* on the world around you or use it *negatively*.

_____

_____

_____

_____

_____

_____

_____

_____

_____

_____

_____

_____

_____

_____

_____

_____

_____

_____

_____

_____

_____

_____

_____

_____

_____

_____

Day 354

Write a Short Story about one day... *only twenty four hours,* of the most trying day you can *remember,* and what it took for you to *make it* through it. Be it life related or *job related* make it *interesting,* write the challenges and *items* you over came from *beginning to end.*

Day 355

Simply just *Wishing for or Wanting* badly for something is *Useless* When There's No Movement...
explain

_____

_____

_____

_____

_____

_____

_____

_____

_____

_____

_____

_____

_____

_____

_____

_____

_____

_____

_____

_____

_____

_____

_____

_____

_____

_____

_____

Day 356

Write a Letter: addressed to you, telling you *exactly* what you think about *your writing skills* after attempting to write for *20 minutes* every day for a year. *Tell yourself* the things you can do *better* and ask yourself *how much* effort did you expel in the process. Write *three goals* you set for the coming year. *Be honest with you.*

when
the weight
of days in your pen
is heavier than your arms
will allow you to lift
when you think and move
at the same time
but you are
directionally challenged
when you know
those you helped
will not utter a word
in your defense
when standing alone
is reminiscent
of the duty
of sun and moon
sometimes alone
is how the job is done
when you are more
words than sound
more fight than battle
when you notice
times arrival
weapons drawn
knowing it can't hurt you
if you stay focused
writing is more doing
than don't
more starting
than stop
more corrections
than errors
Keep Writing

Day 357

Write a *Poem:* When You Open *Troubles Door*

_____

_____

_____

_____

_____

_____

_____

_____

_____

_____

_____

_____

_____

_____

_____

_____

_____

_____

_____

_____

_____

_____

_____

_____

_____

_____

_____

Day 358

I discovered after completing *my first book* the *acknowledgement page* offered the biggest challenge. Here you should *start writing* the names of every one you need to give *thanks and appreciation* for. It is easier when you have this done *in advance*

Day 359

Write a Short Story: The Day *I Started Believing* In *Miracles*.

_____
_____
_____
_____
_____
_____
_____
_____
_____
_____
_____
_____
_____
_____
_____
_____
_____
_____
_____
_____
_____
_____
_____
_____
_____
_____
_____
_____
_____

Things 2 Think About

It is time to begin the process of *finalizing the books* you are

constructing

A. Will you include an *introduction*, a *preface* or **both**?

B. How *many pages* will it consist of?

C. Will it be a book of *poetry and short stories* or will you

create *two* separate books.

D. You must find an *editor* to go over your pages, it is easy

to read through them yourself and *miss* the small *errors* be-

cause you are the writer and *your mind* will read what you

thought you wrote.

E. Write on a *separate page* notes to write by or what you

expect to accomplish.

F. *Add a date* you plan to have all the work *completed*.

G. You are a *writer*, writing is a *job* being your own *boss*

means you must be critical of you.

WRITE as if WRITING MATTERS

Day 360

Self analyzation remains *the best way* to insure we are putting out *our best* work. *Write a letter* of self discovery. *'When I Discovered There Was More to Me Than I'*...

_____

_____

_____

_____

_____

_____

_____

_____

_____

_____

_____

_____

_____

_____

_____

_____

_____

_____

_____

_____

_____

_____

_____

_____

Day 361

Write a poem: This is Called *Letting It OUT!*

Day 362

The Very *Next Time* I Find Myself

_____

_____

_____

_____

_____

_____

_____

_____

_____

_____

_____

_____

_____

_____

_____

_____

_____

_____

_____

_____

_____

_____

_____

_____

_____

_____

_____

_____

_____

_____

Day 363

Write a Short Story: If *Her / His* Eyes Were *Bullets*

Day 364

Write the *Pitch* for one of the projects completed here, to get *investors or publishers* interested in *reviewing* your words, books, play or movie treatment.

_____

_____

_____

_____

_____

_____

_____

_____

_____

_____

_____

_____

_____

_____

_____

_____

_____

_____

_____

_____

_____

_____

_____

_____

_____

_____

_____

_____

CONGRATULATIONS! You have arrived at the mountain top.
now it is time to JUMP

Day 365

Free Write: What *Life* has *Taught Me*.

_____

_____

_____

_____

_____

_____

_____

_____

_____

_____

_____

_____

_____

_____

_____

_____

_____

_____

_____

_____

_____

_____

_____

_____

_____

_____

_____

_____

have you
ever rose
early enough
to wake the sun
cut the cards
before the hand
was dealt for the day
went all in, added a
promissory note
for a couple of
tomorrow's
daring Fate
to challenge
your worth?
we are not
in control of much
but every day
Challenge
your worth
time may be
unwilling to pay
what you ask
but if showing up
with a signed request
is the best you can do
Do It!

Before you claim the book a failure or declare it a success:

Welcome to the new era of you : You are a writer, even if you did not complete all of the task included, you have indeed started the process of a *new beginning*. The next few pages will guide you through compiling the information from the book to make some sense out of what you spent a *full year* doing.

There were multiple pages with just the starter kit, a line, a couple words or a title for you to write whatever you deemed necessary to complete the *thought process* on a particular topic. The following pages will help you put together the words you've written if you want to *publish* any of them.

I am grateful you decided to go through this journey with me. I am a true believer if you *train your mind* to look for the greatness in you, it will find it in every corner of your thoughts, staying focused and positive works with you for your good. A *twenty to thirty minute* writing session is just a *warm up*, similar to stretching before exercising. Hopefully you and your mind *worked* that portion out.

It was an honor to have you along for the thought

Thank You awesomely, I am sure you will accomplish more than the *small writing assignments* contained between the covers here. Peace and Blessings.

And As Always... Let Us Write

Children's Book / Fairytale

There maybe portions of the story you have begun to tell that requires your assistance to become a completed thought. *Work on it*, refine the process, read it over and over again, edit to your satisfaction... and you are finished with your Children's Book or Fairytale . Which ever you choose, it is your work and you should be proud.

Here are the days to help you put it all together:

Day 12 - Day 42 - Day 74 - Day 108 - Day 140 - Day 173

Day 206 - Day 235 - Day 264 - Day 291 - Day 321 - Day 350

Remember: practice doesn't make you perfect, it only makes you better... *Work on getting better*. Here you have the makings of a Book for Children no matter what title you give it... The honor of working with you is all mine.

Additional steps or stages:
to extend the story for your children's book or fairytale

13. *Obstacle or Problem 2 for your children's book or fairytale:* identify the item and write how it occurs or under what circumstances it comes about, detail the exact solution the main character and side-kick will use to accomplish the task.

14. *Describe the background* for four main scenes in your children's book or fairytale... give a more *detailed description* as if you were having an artist illustrate or draw it from your words.

15. *Decide* if you want the dream in your children's book or fairytale *to be ferocious, scary or simply an easily solvable* step by step process to guide them through...write the conflict or problem in detail.

Remember: Everything We Do - Can Be Much Better With Practice

Stage Play

Writing a play although not an easy task, comes with terminology and a certain format you must place it in before submitting it to possibly be accepted. ie... *Acts, Set, scenes,* technical requirement's, lighting cues, stage directions (right, left, up, down) just to name a few. It is *important* for your play to be read just as well as acted.

Here are the days to help you assemble the writings for your play:

Day 10 - Day 30 - Day 58 - Day 87 - Day 115 - Day 137

Day 165 - Day 190 - Day - 217 - Day 237 - Day 309

Day 340

Now that you have *completed a few steps* in getting your ideas in order... *what are your plans,* how will you proceed to the next step, how will you go about raising your Play writing skills to the *next level?*

Every dream starts with eyes open, attempting to remember what parts to write down. *Write everything down,* try and recall *every word,* the way the room was decorated, *the color* of the table settings, even the taste of the dessert. You are a Play Write.... *Remember like it.*

Hopefully the *process or technique* you gained from following the few steps in the book will *help you* understand there is *so much to see,* when you are *out and about,* maybe you will watch closer as you board the next *plane or train... your next visit* to the groceries, the mall, train your eyes to *remember.*

Thank you for the *ride along,* it is time you begin the *journey by yourself.* I am grateful you *took the time* to join me in the adventure. Be *awesome* always... and *write about it...*

Your book of short stories can have any title you choose to place on the cover. You can create it in any format, include pictures if you like. Each short story can be submitted for publishing in various publications and magazines. ***Congratulations*** on writing your thoughts.

Here are the Days Your Short Stories appear:

Day 5 - Day 34 - Day 38 - Day 60 - Day 69 - Day 89

Day 93 - Day 101 - Day 111 - Day 122 - Day 148

Day 162 - Day 184 - Day 188 - Day 193 - Day 200

Day 203 - Day 209 - Day 220 - Day 245 - Day 256

Day 265 - Day 280 - Day 287 - Day 298 - Day 308

Day 310 - Day 327 - Day 342 - Day 351 - Day 353

Day 354 - Day 359 - Day 363

Re read your stories, check for ***punctuation*** and spelling errors. You have so many options, why not choose ***option E, ALL the Above***?

I Thank You for giving something new and different ***a chance***. ***Practice*** your ***skills daily,*** you will be surprised at the things your pen will create. The mind is a ***muscle*** similar to abs… if you do not exercise it - it can get all out of shape too.

You should be Proud of yourself. I am proud of you for sure.

Poetry

Poetry is considered the quintessential language of love... well maybe not, but I would like to think so.

There are as **many forms of poetry** as there are languages; **well almost**, your style is perfect. **Write**. There were titles, short phrases and lines on pages used to spark your **creative juices**, you could turn any of them into whatever you like, **even a poem** if you felt just so.

Here is a list of the pages where poems were expected:

Day 3 - Day - Day 11 - Day 17 - Day 18 - Day 22 - Day 25

Day 28 - Day 33 - Day 40 - Day 43 - Day 54 - Day 70

Day 78 - Day 79 - Day 83 - Day 99 - Day 109 - Day 116

Day 128 - Day 138 - Day 143 Day - 150 - Day 171

Day 177 - Day 179 - Day 183 - Day 186 - Day 187

Day 195 - Day 198 - Day 214 - Day 221 - Day 232

Day 246 - Day 261 - Day 277 - Day 312 - Day 317

Day 324 - Day 329 - Day 333 - Day 338 - Day 352

Day 357 - Day 361

I believe in editing poetry for thoughts sake, at *first read* the words may feel comfortable, *second read* you find ownership in their placement, *third read* places the verses to rest on your tongue. *Edit your work,* and your words, *to insure* they sound as great as you would want them to sound and be read.

Thank You for sharing *your time* with the thoughts on these pages. I am sure the book or books *you create* from your words will be beneficial to every person who makes a *purchase*, and discover the *blessings* contained within.

Well it is not a complete movie **as of yet**, but it is the beginning **treatment** for the final script. Of all the genre's of writing, movie scripting is probably the most complicated. Don't let a small thing like complications deter you from your goal. This book was considered complicated at first, **but like practice does** it makes us better at complicated matters.

Putting your thoughts together **in line** with a projected script was our goal, **and here we are**... I wanted to present you with a **starter kit** for your creative thoughts to know where **home is**, and where the door leading to outside was located. **Completing everything is a celebration**, completing anything is a celebration too. So here we will spend a couple of seconds **celebrating** then - **back to the matter at hand.**

Here are the pages of thoughts for your Movie Treatment:

Day 7 - Day 32 - Day 61 - Day 84 - Day 105 - Day 135

Day 169 - Day 196 - Day 224 - Day 243 - Day 251

Day 283 - Day 300 - Day 331

There is so much **more to learn**... making it this far you **know** now, learning is fundamental in accomplishing anything you set your mind to. **You are a Writer... Write... Write everything** and anything you want... **create** your own style, **add words weekly** to your vocabulary and you will find a new style in your fingers automatically.

You are awesome, you are great

Thank you for joining me on this journey of New...

Peace and Blessings

Additional Products by: AJ Houston

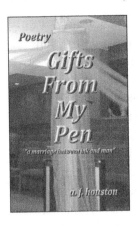

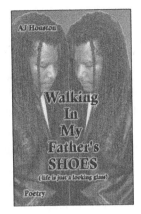

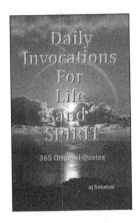

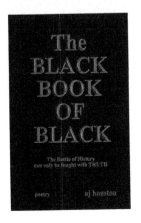

New Titles Coming Soon
Not Yet Lost Jan 2016
F.A.C.E. June 2016
(Fibromyalgia Awareness Changes Everything)
The Legend of Shrenk July 2016
Lost Pens
(A Pocket Guide for Writers)
*all books can be purchased @ amazon.com, cre-
atespace, or at the next performance to receive a per-
sonalized signature. Booking and contact information
can be located on the last page of this book.*

Let Us Write
Acknowledgements

Thank You: Birdie L. Houston, Jimmie Jay Houston, Geneva Conner, Ruben S, Conner I, Booker Green, Shirley Green, Jeffrey Phillips, Zetha l. Phillips, Mother Willis, Moma Vinne, Moma Mary, Josephine Kelley, Cedric green, Helen Green, Bro. & Sis Boles, Tony Evans, R.T. Johnson, Oretha Johnson, Peace Maker, Richard I Stuckey, Lemuel Isreal, Buddy Straus, Jimmy Houston, Jacque Lacy, Kimberly Johnson, Tracy Wynn, Timothy Johnson, Shanttel, Shayla, Brittany, Nicholas, Dominique, Alexander, Jimmie II, Prophet, Mirror, Butta, Shanesse, Valerie, Deborah, Stephanie, Felicia, Algenise, Fonda, Shannon, Beverly, Patricia, Camille, Cynthia, Steve, Andre, Charlotte, Clifton, Sherita, Don Juan, Janean, Jahmal, Kara, Anthony, Giselle, Natty, Hadji, Will, Darius, A.P., Deidre, Angel, Stacy, Adiah, Michael, Bee Wisely, Donna, Donya, Jan, Audrey, Yoland, Vernell, Edith Jean, Nelda, Aunt Pat, Aunt Jean, Tony, Mary Ann, Pinky, Dale, Barbara, Amanda, Tino, Tonya, Demonte, Carla, Phillip, Natasha, Carl, Jorell, Andre, Tremel, Kay, Keheri, Christpher, Prudence, Candy, Masterpiece, Whisper, Gwen, Elyse, Herbert, Larry, Pamela, Mr. Robinson, Rodney, Pamela, Mike, Chantal, Faye Marie… the hardest thing about giving thanks is someone will always feel left out… as to not leave anyone out… I Thank all those who know me, who met me somewhere I may not remember, those I know well that I can't remember at this time… Honestly, I am grateful and honored by all who has graced my space, to all the contributors of my earned patience… Thank You All for the Love…

To: Mr. Brentom (Chuck) Jackson a special Thanks for helping me with finishing up this book…

To: J a very special Thanks for listening to each and every prompt. Those are Best Friends type qualities.

To: Lewis Allen for his contributions were instrumental also…

Thanks to Shazz Raymond for lending me her eyes for the front and back cover, their pupils have become excellent students to finding the hidden beauty this world has to offer. Photos by Shazz

About the Author

 To my son's and daughters who have all at one time or another wrote just to see how pens felt caressed by their fingers. To my friends most of them are poets who think writing is an exercise of necessity, for an upcoming project or performance, a wedding in the wings or a funeral. Writing is exercise for writers attempting to build strength of thought, in thinking, of processing images into sound.

Born *Albert Jeffrey Houston*, growing up everyone called him Jeff and now goes by AJ, a Resident of Fort Worth, Texas by way of Dallas, Texas. Father, Author, Poet, Motivational Speaker, Event Coordinator and Host, Creative Writing Facilitator and Founder of the Psychology of Writing Institute. He believes writing is fun to mental, it is the exercise of the mind. He prides himself in the ability to connect to youth in workshops, no matter the setting. Believes he can sing at least a little bit.

The important things are his seeds, trying to reconnect with his daughters Shanttel and Shayla whom he loves dearly and stay connected with other loves of his life in this order Tremel, Brittany, Nicholas, Dominique, Alexander, Jimmie II… family is of the greatest importance, how can you show love and respect to teach youth you don't know if you do not love and respect your own first. Words are a gift that must be shared and practiced to become skillful. Pens are weapons when used incorrectly.

He has friends from his time of military service that still bare the title of best. Richard Isaac and Lemuel, they remain a constant source of support and inspiration to this day. His motto is *"every day you must be at your best to become better at being your best".*

Write with respect for the art
practice writing for the love of words.

Contact Information:

njalphabets.org

www.twitter.com/ajwordartist

www.facebook.com/ajhouston

www.youtube.com/ajhouston

www.reverbnation.com/ajhouston

ajwordartist@gmail.com

instagram.com/ajwordartist

Additional Products:

CD 's Love Seasons - The Awakening - Whispers

Books Coming Soon

The Legend of Shrenk

Not Yet Lost

F. A. C. E.
(Fibromyalgia Awareness Changes Everything)

Lost Pens
(A Pocket Guide For Writers)

T-Shirts

Poetic Lessons

NJA Gear

For Booking: **Contact**

AJ Houston

@ **poetajhouston@gmail.com**

Made in the USA
Middletown, DE
22 January 2023

21642973R00225